**Better Homes and Gardens**®

# a season to celebrate

our Christmas legends, customs, and beliefs

From our hearts to yours,
a unique collection of cards and gifts
for your home and family from the editors of
*Better Homes and Gardens*®.

©1997 Meredith Corporation. All rights reserved. Printed in U.S.A.

Produced by Meredith Custom Publishing, 1912 Grand Avenue, Des Moines, Iowa 50309-3379
Library of Congress Catalog Number: 97-71057
ISBN: 0-696-20755-9

SENIOR EDITOR:
Pamela Johnson

DESIGN DIRECTOR:
Jann Williams

PROJECT EDITOR:
Lisa Kingsley

DESIGNERS:
Joe Peter Wysong, Chris Conyers, Chad Johnston

MARKETING DIRECTOR:
Hugh Kennedy

PRODUCTION MANAGER:
Ivan McDonald

MANAGING EDITOR:
Deb Gore Ohrn

EDITOR-IN-CHIEF:
Don Johnson

PUBLISHER:
Jack Griffin

HALLMARK CARDS, INC.:
Karen McKernan
Carol Marsh
Tara Pfeifer
Marianne James
Nancy Pretz
Dorothy Haws-Dibenedetto

MEREDITH PUBLISHING GROUP
President, Publishing Group: Christopher M. Little
Vice President and Publishing Director: John P. Loughlin

MEREDITH CORPORATION
Chairman: Jack D. Rehm
President and Chief Executive Officer: William T. Kerr

I will honor  Christmas in my heart,  and try to keep  it all the year.

—*Charles Dickens*, A Christmas Carol, *1843*

table of contents

## a season to celebrate

our Christmas legends, customs, and beliefs

# 'tis the season

The holiday season works a kind of magic on us all.

Jim Howard, a writer for Hallmark, recalls a seasonal epiphany of his boyhood that was transformative, one that remains with him still.

"It didn't happen every Christmas morning," he writes, "but I know it happened at least once, because the memory still shows me waking up with that wild surge of child-energy, before anyone else in the house was awake, and dashing out to the living room.

"It was just daybreak—enough darkness to shroud the glowing tree, rising from a heap of gifts, in mystery; enough light to see that, outside the window, our street was asleep in the perfect silence of newfallen snow.

"The hardwood floor was cold under my bare feet, but I was lit up from inside, ablaze with delight, absolutely alive.

"And now, more clearly than all memories relived on many Christmases since then—the mad joy of plunging into presents and stockings, or lavish family feasts that sprawl into the heavy sweetness of idle afternoons—I remember that moment.

"Surely I was the luckiest child ever born, standing breathless at the center of the world, where all its rich and unknown treasures lay."

The reason for the season is embodied in that instant. But the glowing tree, the presents, the stockings, the feasts, are all agents of celebration; they create the atmosphere in which we experience moments that change us forever.

In *A Season to Celebrate: Our Christmas Legends, Customs, and Beliefs*, Hallmark Cards and *Better Homes and Gardens*® join forces to explore the history of the rituals and the truth behind the legends of the Christmas season.

Though each of our individual celebrations is different in its way, there are traditions we share—a common language we speak during this season of hope, renewal, celebration, and joy.

Hallmark and *Better Homes and Gardens*® are keepers of the flame that is our collective holiday tradition. Gather round it, be warmed by it, be enlightened by it. Because to know a tradition is to keep it.

adornment

So now is come our joyfulst feast; let every man be jolly.

Each room with ivy leaves is dressed and every post with holly.

—George Wither, 16th century English poet

When the snow piles up during the coldest, grayest days of winter, the scent of fresh evergreens warms the senses and soothes the soul.

The tradition of decking the halls with greenery, colorful and fragrant fruit, and flowers, dried and fresh, is perhaps the oldest Christmas tradition of them all. It dates, in fact, to a time when Christmas didn't yet exist in any form.

During a midwinter celebration called Saturnalia, ancient Romans draped evergreens such as pine and fir in door- ways, windows, and fireplaces. The aromatic branches were thought to bring luck and fertility throughout the year. The fact that they stayed green and seemingly full of eternal life made them all the more magical.

Because holly, too—with its green, spiky leaves and bright red berries— kept its color and thrived through bitter winters, medieval people believed it possessed great magical powers. Primitive people hung holly above doorways to entice woodland spirits into their homes during the winter solstice.

In Victorian times in America, holly adorned almost every house at holiday-time. Shaped into wreaths and swags, holly hung above door- ways, wrapped around banisters, or formed center- pieces on dining tables. The prettiest sprig of holly with the most brilliant berries was always reserved for the top of the Christmas pudding.

Though it lacks holly's red berry, the graceful, climbing vine of ivy— thought to bring fruitfulness—was another holiday favorite. Although the Church of England frowned upon ivy as pagan, parishioners were more open-minded.

Over the centuries, though, pagan and Christian traditions became as intertwined as a garland of greenery around a banister. The love of old-world traditions and the Victorian love for ornamentation was not to be suppressed. Together, they finally brought greens into Americans' homes for good.

While children may have waited eagerly each year for their first glimpse of the tree, it was mistletoe that interested older revelers. For more than a century, mistletoe has sparked spontaneous kisses from even the most timid among us. At holiday parties, when Christmas tree lights bathe the room in color and carols resound throughout the house, a sprig of mistletoe hanging from an archway tempts mischievous romancers to share a kiss or two.

To the Romans, mistletoe symbolized peace. When opposing warriors met beneath it, they laid down their arms, kissed, and declared a truce until the next day.

The much-loved mistletoe "kissing ball," however, was created by the English in the 1800s, and they surrounded it with superstition. It

was said a lady kissed under the ribboned cluster of heavy, coarse leaves and shiny berries was lucky indeed. Any girl not kissed was destined to remain single for another year.

"And who is she," chimes an old English ballad, "that will not allow a kiss claimed under the mistletoe bough?"

Indeed, decorating the house with greenery each year fills it with an air of revelry and celebration. It invites the "height of the Christmas spirit to linger over" us, as a Pennsylvania man writes. But, too, he suggests, there is comfort as well as joy in the ritual of adornment.

"The first Saturday of every December finds me with a bevy of friends decorating in earnest," he

writes. We hang evergreen wreaths on the front door and windows. Candles follow on the windowsills.

"A fresh garland, stuffed with ivy and fresh herbs and secured with red satin ribbons, appears on the walnut staircase. Boughs of hemlock, cedar, and holly from the yard decorate the mantels in the living room, dining room, and kitchen, and crown the mirror over the cherry sideboard. The Victorian carolers are reinstated on the living room mantel. The train set awaits its circular journey in the living room."

> "The first Saturday of every December finds me with a bevy of friends decorating in earnest."

His home shines with light and life for the three weeks before Christmas Eve—mirroring the adornment nature bestowed on the earth on a Christmas Eve he fondly recalls.

"The fire dies down. I throw a jacket over my shoulders and walk into the yard. Snow frosts the boughs of the ancient hemlocks— the moon on the snow burns like a fire opal. A star catches a cloud and cuts it in two, and at that moment," he writes, "Christmas Day slips in unnoticed."

Bring forth the holly,
the box, and the bay.
Deck out our cottage
for glad Christmas Day.

—*Traditional English verse*

Now Christmas comes

leafy and floral,

Poinsettia, pine,

the mountain laurel.

Now wreaths of fir,

of spruce or pine

hang on the door

with a green shine.

—*Paul Engle*

At Christmas time…

...We deck the hall

With holly branches

Brave and tall,

With sturdy pine and

Hemlock bright,

And in the Yule log's

Dancing light

We tell old tales of

Field and fight

At Christmas time.

—*Traditional English verse*

The dark night wakes

...the glory breaks, and Christmas comes once more.

—From "O Little Town of Bethlehem" by Phillips Brooks, 1835-1893

# light

Sing, ye heavens, tell the story, Of his glory, Till his praises Flood with light earth's darkest places!

—*Philipp Nicolai*

Christmas is at its heart a celebration of the birth of the Light of the World. That, in concert with the fact that it falls during the darkest time of the year, makes for a season suffused with light.

As the shadows lengthen and the days grow shorter, a beacon of hope transcends the dim pall of winter—and it happens at the same time each year among people of different faiths and ethnic origins. The candles, lanterns, and "stars" of both religious and secular tradition cast a new light across the land, brightening our emotional land-scapes as well. In winter's darkest hour, light's shimmering power to renew is proven year after year— warming hearts and restoring spirits.

Whether it's from votives tucked into holiday greens or Hanukkah lamps blazing in a menorah, the flicker of candlelight signals the season. December wouldn't be the same without it.

Yet for all its timeless ritual and symbolic meaning, candlelight no longer is alone in announcing winter's arrival. In the United States, the season is heralded by electric lights—white or multicolored, blinking or static, in strings or inside figurines. We drape strand after strand on our homes, buildings, and landscapes in blinding abundance.

Although its origins date back to winter solstice celebrations of pagan times, the practice of celebrating the season with light took on religious significance as Judaism and Christianity developed. In the Jewish faith, Hanukkah commemo-rates the first recorded battle for religious freedom. The lighting of the menorah celebrates the miracle of the Temple of Jerusalem's lamps, which burned for eight days on only a small supply of sanctified oil.

Christians share a similar custom with the lighting of Advent candles. Advent means "a coming" and refers

to the Messiah's arrival on Christmas Day. The religious observance takes place during the four weeks before Christmas, when Christians prepare for the celebration of Christ's birth.

The Moravians—a religious sect whose members immigrated to this country from Germany in the 18th century—prepare for Christmas by handmaking hundreds of candles from molds that belonged to their ancestors, in anticipation of their shimmering Christmas Eve service.

The magical effect of so many candles is powerful enough to light an elderly Moravian woman's memory of the Christmas Eves of her girlhood, one of which she fondly reflects upon in a 1948 edition of the *Iowa Outpost*.

"From behind a screen where someone had been busy lighting the tapers, [a young couple] brought what looked like a tray load of blossoms, and children gave an ecstatic sigh at the sight of all those wavering tiny flames," she writes. "The couple started down the aisle, he carrying the board with a great show of caution while she, smiling, put the candles into outstretched hands, whispering something gracious, warning children not to get them too close to clothing or hair.

After this, the minister gave a brief talk about the Light of the World, while dreamy eyes looked into the flames, and heads turned so that eyes could see the room alive with candle glow. When we were told to put out our lights, carefully, one row at a time, there was much puffing and much sniffling for the blended fragrance of wax and evergreen. Then, while the smoke wisps faded on the air, we rose for the last hymn, 'Joy to the World,' for the benediction. For us, it was the climax of the whole Christmas season."

In sunny Mexico, light is prized no less than in the Moravian settlements of Iowa, Pennsylvania, and North Carolina, as a vital element of the Christmas celebration.

"When we were told to put out our lights, carefully, one row at a time, there was much puffing and much sniffling for the blended fragrance of wax and evergreen."

The tradition of luminarias grew bright there, where candles glowing in sand-weighted bags line the streets for Christmas processionals. Today, people in cities and towns across America have adopted the custom by turning their own streets and sidewalks into pathways of brilliant light.

Whether we kindle a flame—or even fire up some holiday wattage just for fun—the radiance of the holiday season endures.

In the darkest days of winter, for many of us a simple flicker of light has the power to renew our weary spirits and give us hope for brighter days to come.

Candle, candle,

Burning bright

On our window

Sill tonight,

Like the

shining Christmas star

Guiding shepherds

From afar,

Lead some weary

Traveler here,

That he may share

Our Christmas cheer.
—*Isabel Shaw*

dle will be blessed if He goes by

—*Aileen Fisher*

Now when Jesus was born in Bethlehem of Judaea

in the days of Herod the King,

behold, there came wise men

# worship

from the east to Jerusalem, saying,

where is he that is born King of the Jews?

For we have seen his star in the east,

and are come to worship him.

*—Matthew 2:1-2*

Morning Star, O cheering sight! Ere thou cam'st,

fill my heart

how dark the night!

Jesus mine, in me shine,

with light divine.

—Aileen Fisher

Somewhere amidst the hustle and bustle of Christmas shopping, gift-wrapping, cookie-baking, and parties, many of us slow down long enough to attend a church service or gather the family at home for some quiet contemplation during the holiday season.

**W**e are of different denominations and religious traditions. We worship in tiny white churches in the country and big stone cathedrals in the city, but our purpose is the same: to unhurry our minds, take on an attitude of prayerfulness, and reflect upon the true meaning and wonder of the season. When we worship, we are remembering that "Christmas" springs from "Christ mass" and that "holiday" springs from "holy day."

For those of the Catholic faith, Midnight Mass on Christmas Eve is undoubtedly the most stirring service of the Christmas season.

Mass is usually celebrated at midnight on Christmas Eve because it is believed that is the hour that Christ was born. However, in the Southwest states bordering Mexico, Catholic churches sometimes hold mass at dawn, just as the sun is beginning to rise and bathe the earth in warmth and light.

To believers, Christmas truly is a season—and not just one determined by commerce. Advent is a sacred season comprising the four weeks before Christmas Day.

The celebration revolves around an Advent wreath that consists of four candles—one for each week—encircled by greenery. One candle is lit the first Sunday of Advent and an additional one each week thereafter until, on Christmas Eve,

the wreath is a luminous and glowing testament to the nearness of the birth of Christ.

Not every church-going family celebrates Advent at home, but most churches do. Advent services have a particular air of expectancy and joy about them. There is almost always special music of the season—a Christmas cantata of sacred music by the choir or simply joyful singing by the congregation—and there are special programs.

The most enchanting of these is usually the Christmas pageant, the time-honored tradition of reenacting the Nativity with children dressed in costume as Mary, Joseph, the shepherds and Wise Men, and sometimes, as some of the more humble creatures who made their beds in the stable that night. Even the tiniest children sing songs and give recitations—often punctuated by tender and loving laughter from the audience.

"A piece had to be learned for the Christmas program at Merrill's Grove Baptist Church, and I was admonished not to twist the hem of my skirt to immodest heights while delivering it," writes Julie McDonald in an essay called "The Lesser Christmas Miracle" in the book, *Christmas in the Midwest.* "I performed without a lapse of memory and left my hemline alone, and when the program was over, we all got brown paper bags filled with hard candy. The bumpy raspberries with soft centers were my favorites, but I also admired the small rounds with a flower that remained visible until the candy was sucked to a sliver."

"Now on Christmas Eve the children came into their own," recalls another woman in a half-century-old magazine article. "The 'exercises' were theirs, and they were the usual thing: much singing, much speaking, solos or in concert. The mistakes were theirs too: a letter in the Merry Christmas legend held upside down; a verse spoken out of turn; too quick or too tardy an entrance into dialog [*sic*], if anything

…"A piece had to be learned for the Christmas program at Merrill's Grove Baptist Church, and I was admonished not to twist the hem of my skirt to immodest heights while delivering it."…

so advanced as a dialog was a program feature. People liked that sort of thing, but the costuming was the despair of those who coached the children…To dress boys as shepherds was…a problem. In later years bathrobes solved that one. The program committee felt reasonably sure that the [shepherds] wore bathrobes or something similar."

Christmas pageants are rarely flawless by this world's standards, but certainly, when performed in the spirit of worship, they are perfect in the eyes of heaven.

The angels wings

is [*sic*] white as snow,

# O, white as snow,

white as snow.
—*Langston Hughes*

# father

# Christmas

His eyes—how they twinkled!

His dimples, how merry.

His cheeks were like Roses,

his nose like a cherry!

—*C. Clement Moore*, "The Visit of St. Nicholas"

One of the most endearing images of Christmas is that of cherry-cheeked Old St. Nick, the North Pole-dwelling fellow who provides the incentive to be good and delivers the reward for having done so.

Christmas wouldn't be the same without him. Clad cheerily in red, his roly-poly image adorns everything from holiday greeting cards to fireside stockings. And for good reason. Santa's twinkling high spirits, love of children, and open-armed giving deliver an important message to us all.

The persona of the Santa Claus we know and love has origins in a real person—St. Nicholas of Myra, a 4th-century Christian bishop who was born in Patara, Turkey. The story goes that he dropped gold coins down the chimney of a poor widower who had three daughters and no dowries. The coins fell into the toes of stockings the girls had hung from the chimney

to dry. The coins were more than enough to create respectable dowries, the daughters married, and everyone lived happily ever after.

St. Nicholas of Myra's evolution into Santa Claus of the North Pole was a gradual one. St. Nicholas died on or about December 6, 343 A.D. More than six centuries later, Vladimir of Russia went to Constantinople and carried back with him tales of Nicholas. Stories of St. Nicholas spread to the nomadic people who followed their reindeer herds around the North Pole.

European countries began adopting and adapting St. Nicholas to their own cultures. Among early Dutch settlers in America, Sint Nikalaus evolved into Santa Nikalaus and, finally, Santa Claus.

Dutch children traditionally set out their wooden shoes filled

with carrots for Santa's reindeer, in hopes he would fill them with toys and goodies. The work of two Americans—Dr. Clement Moore, author of the poem "The Visit of St. Nicholas," and Thomas Nast, who first illustrated Santa Claus in *Harper's Illustrated Weekly* in 1863 forever etched the image of Santa Claus into our hearts and minds.

For the nation's children, Santa Claus is far more than an image on a page. He is as real as the snow that falls on Christmas Eve. And if there are doubts that creep in, there are always the believers who keep the faith.

A Pennsylvania mother recalls a Christmas when her daughter was small and

her beloved teddy bear, "T-Bar," was so threadbare it was too fragile to wash.

As Christmas approached, she and her husband tried to convince their daughter that Santa would be happy to bring her a fine new T-Bar.

"I don't want a new bear," she said. "Santa will just have to make him a new coat."

The woman and her husband started a cross-country search for a brown bear exactly like the old one. There were bears like their daughter's available, but none in brown.

> "I don't want a new bear," she said. "Santa will just have to make him a new coat."

"What if Santa brought you a pink or a blue T Bar?" she asked her daughter. "Oh, no! Santa knows that T-Bar is brown," she replied with confidence.

With only a week left, the little girl's father called the company

headquarters in New Jersey. Yes, they did have brown bears somewhere, but they didn't sell to individuals, just to stores—in bulk.

"Anxiety filled me," the woman writes. "My little girl's dream was going to be shattered. Then, miraculously, on Christmas Eve a gift arrived. Inside we found a brand-new *brown* T-Bar. Our only clue to the sender was the package's New Jersey postmark."

That night, the little girl put the old T-Bar on the floor near the door. "I love you, T-Bar," she said confidently. "Santa will come tonight and fix your torn coat; you will be like new again. Don't be afraid."

The next morning, the house awoke to the little girl's shrieks of joy.

"Christmas proceeded with the usual cheer," the woman recalls. "But somehow, the biblical message, 'Unless you become as little children, you shall not enter into the kingdom of heaven,' became more real for all of us that day, taught to us by our faithful little girl, her brown bear, and a thoughtful stranger."

Backward, turn backward

o time in your flight;

Make me a child again

just for tonight.
—*Elizabeth Akers Allen*

A good time is coming,

I wish it were here,

the very best time

in the whole time of year;

I'm counting each day

on my fingers and thumbs

—the week that must pass

before Santa Claus comes.

*—Author unknown*

Old Santa is an active man,
He glides down chimneys black...

...Fills stockings while his reindeer wait,
and then goes dashing back!

—*Lois Lenski*

He comes in the night! He comes in the night! He softly, silently comes,

while the little brown heads on the pillow so white are dreaming of bugles and drums.

*—Anonymous, 1880*

A Christmas thought for someone

who is busy all the year

Doing good for other folks

and spreading joy and cheer

# greetings

To hope that Christmas Day

and every day the whole year through

Will help repay you in a way

by being good to you.

*—Christmas Greetings to the Pastor, a 1930 Hallmark Christmas card*

Christmas cards are magical missives, wingless angels that bear messages of joy, hope, and news of those we hold dear. As we sit by the wintertime hearth to write addresses and affix stamps, thoughts of family and friends warm us and refresh a thousand memories.

A s the holidays draw near, we listen carefully for the rattle of the mail carrier at the mailbox, inspect envelopes for postmarks, familiar or foreign, and open each card to let the spirit of the season unfold in our homes.

The ritual of writing notes that carry holiday sentiments to loved ones dates back to ancient times. The Egyptians and Romans seemingly sent along handwritten greetings with their New Year's gifts. But the tradition of sending printed Christmas cards has been around only since London businessman Henry Cole sent the first one in 1843.

Fearing that he would not have time to visit all of his friends personally at Christmastime, Cole asked John Holcott Horsley, an artist in the Royal Academy, to design a card conveying his Christmas wishes. The card Horsley designed is thought to be the first commercially printed Christmas card.

The English custom of sending holiday greeting cards spread slowly to America. For more than 30 years, the only Christmas cards available in this country were imported.

But in 1875, German immigrant Louis Prang of Boston began publishing an American version of the popular English missives. Known as the "Father of the Christmas Card," Prang perfected the process of multicolor printing in the 1870s. His cards were works of art, often incorporating as many as 20 different colors. He also popularized the use of religious motifs in his holiday greetings.

Prang's artful cards established the basis for much of the Christmas-card tradition in the United States.

"Wornout [sic] from choosing gifts [for old friends and schoolmates]," wrote a woman in the late 19th century, "we usually fall back on Christmas cards, which constitute one of the most precious and at the same time inexpensive contributions of these latter days to the neglected cause of sentiment."

In the 1890s, the penny-postcard craze hit America, and by the turn of the century, inexpensive German-made postcards flooded the market. Although the cards were crude, the price was right.

For the next 20 years, German-made penny postcards were the greeting of choice—until they were banned during World War I. The American greeting-card industry would flourish again, however, led by an ambitious young man named Joyce Hall, who founded Hallmark Cards in Kansas City in 1910.

Young Mr. Hall said that "postcards were not really a means of communication between people. Most of them were either humorous or simply decorative and lacked a from-me-to-you sentiment; they were sent because it was the thing to do."

He felt the thing to do was to incite a renaissance in civility. Greeting cards, Hall believed, "were more than a form of communication—they were a social custom."

Christmas cards have always expressed traditional sentiments concerning the timeless spirit of the season, but they have almost always been underpinned by themes that have mirrored the happenings of the times.

During the Depression, cards often expressed faith that better times were ahead. Patriotic themes wished soldiers home for the holidays during World War II. The flag—often carried by Santa—brought the colors of red, white, and blue to the traditional red and green of Christmas. Special cards were created for servicemen overseas. "Across the

> Greeting cards, Hall believed, "were more than a form of communication—they were a social custom."

miles" and "missing you" sentiments reflected the somber reality of the day.

The Christmas-card custom has weathered war, economic turmoil, and social changes spanning far more than a century. It serves the timeless human need to stay in touch, to share one's life with friends and family far and near during the holiday season.

The cards themselves have come a long way since 1843. The designs are more sophisticated, and production processes have been refined. But the message on Henry Cole's first Christmas card is as relevant today as it was then, and will be 100 Christmases from now: "A Merry Christmas and a Happy New Year to You."

I find nothing so dear as that which is given me.

—*Montagne*

"I thought last year would be the end of the Christmas card mania, but I don't think so now. Why, four years ago a Christmas card was a ra

hing. The public then got the mania and the business seems to be getting larger every year. I don't know what we will do if it keeps on."

*—postal official, as quoted in the Washington Star in 1882*

# gifts

. . . they presented unto him gifts; gold,

and frankincense,

and myrrh.

*—The Gospel According to St. Matthew, 2:11*

"Bearing gifts, we traverse afar," was the song of the Magi as they ambled on camelback across the desert to bring gold, frankincense, and myrrh to the Christ Child.

Today, we take planes, trains, and minivans packed with gaily wrapped packages to our Christmas celebrations, but the intention of the gift itself—to give joy and express gratitude—is much the same as it was that ancient night the three wise men were guided by a star.

Gift-giving at the beginning of a new year is a tradition that pre-dates Christmas. Exchanging presents during this time was an old Roman custom called *strenae*. As tokens of their good wishes for the coming year, people gave the gift of "honeyed" pastries to make life sweeter; lamps for a bright future; and precious stones and silver and gold coins to provide for the recipient's wants in the coming year.

Today, the tangible gift inside the box may be a doll, a book, or a pretty hand-knit sweater, but what we are truly bestowing in those brightly wrapped packages is love.

A story shared by a Midwestern man demonstrates that sometimes the humblest gifts are the best gifts of all.

"Christmas last year yielded the usual cache of nice, thoughtful gifts. But the best was a spontaneous gesture," he recalls. "It's an old barn lantern that once lighted the way for a young farmer. That young man, Ollie Bergeland, went on to become a minister and counselor. He and his wife, Ida, were like surrogate grandparents when my brothers and I were growing up. Ollie was our father's professional mentor and a lifelong source of cheer and encouragement—a joyful embodiment of optimism.

"During a holiday visit with Ida, now widowed, she talked about moving to an apartment and wanting to find homes for some of Ollie's things. When she offered me his lantern, I wasn't prepared for my own reaction. Throat tight, eyes welling, it was difficult just to say thanks—or, at the time, to understand why thanks seemed so inadequate. Such lanterns go cheaply enough at any farm sale. But this wasn't just a keepsake …It was part of his life, something he had used and relied upon, something he needed

I shake-shake, shake-shake, shake the package well. But what there is inside of it,

  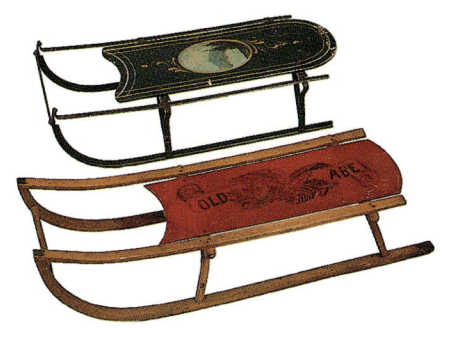 

in the frosty dark of farm work in the days before the rural electric cooperatives brightened the Midwestern landscape. From that farm, he was destined to become a guiding light for so many people, and this old lantern once lighted his way…

"To honor symbols of [people's] lives is a gift we can give to those who have gone on. Ollie may not be with us, but his influence is, and his light. What a wonderful, radiant gift."

Each Christmas we are encouraged, as St. Matthew said, to "give freely, as ye have been freely given." We take stock of our blessings and

attempt to give something back to our families, our friends, our communities. In the days of Rome, the rich in particular were encouraged to share with the poor.

Some things never change. It is unlikely that the breathless anticipation with which the opening of Christmas gifts is awaited by anxious children will ever abate. It is unlikely that it will ever be more exciting to receive a gift than it is to give one. And it is unlikely that we will ever cease to find the greatest and purest joy in giving much to those who have the least.

*"To honor symbols of [people's] lives is a gift we can give to those who have gone on."*

Christmas is, after all, a celebration of its founder, whose spirit moves us to think of others.

In Poland, it is said that Christmas gifts come from the stars in the heavens; in Hungary, from the angels above; and in much of the world, from a jolly old elf named St. Nick. But no matter where they are given or what they happen to be, when they are bestowed with a generous spirit, they always come from the heart.

*shaking will not tell.*
—*James S. Trippett*

Give a little love
to a child,
and you get
a great deal back.

—*John Ruskin*

A bundle is a funny thing, it always set me wondering; for whether it is thin or wide you never know just what's inside.

—*John Farrar*

# songs

Oh, he did whistle and she did sing, and all the bells on earth did ring . . .

*—From an old English carol*

"I always give myself a Christmas present," wrote renowned 19th-century preacher Edward Everett Hale. "And on this particular year the present was a Carol party, which is about as good fun, all things consenting kindly, as a man can have."

He was describing a Christmas Eve when he rented "a span of good horses and a sleigh that I could pack sixteen small children into, tightly stowed." He dashed off "under the full moon, on the snow still white," to serenade citizens of the children's choosing beneath the frosted windows of Boston. "The instant the horses' bells stopped, [the children's] voices began," he wrote, "singing with all that unconscious pathos with which children do sing, and starting tears in your eyes in the midst of your gladness."

Reverend Hale's spirited Christmas Eve sleigh ride is caroling as we best like to imagine it. It also represents caroling come full circle. Originally a ring dance celebrating winter solstice, the carol has a lusty, pagan exuberance that caused early Christian clerics to label the songs "slings of the devil."

Carol lyrics, charged the clerics, were "worldly or worse." Guzzling wassail and ale and moonlit sport with maidens are recurring themes of early carols, and the church lost no time in banning such songs. But the beautiful carol melodies and hearty refrains refused to die.

In the spirit of joining what one can't suppress, St. Francis of Assisi adopted carols for use in a Christmas Eve midnight Mass early in the 13th century, after replacing bawdy lyrics with sacred revisions and inventions. And so pagan mirth was mixed, for the first time, with Christian devotion. The result has created some of the most exuberant and memorable music of all time.

There is another story of the genesis of the carol. According to Christian legend, angels burst into song

while proclaiming the Nativity to shepherds, thus spontaneously composing and performing the first Christmas carol: "Gloria in Excelsis."

Solstice feasts, St. Francis, and choirs of angels have all conspired to make caroling a universal expression of seasonal cheer. Perhaps the most beloved Christmas song of all time, though, is one that is decidedly sacred.

In 1818, the organ of the little church of Oberndorf, Austria, had become unfit for use in the last days before Christmas. This greatly troubled the parish priest, Father Josef Mohr, who wished for music for the Midnight Mass. On the day before Christmas Eve, he was

called to administer the last rites to a dying woman. It was late when he began his walk home, and as he paused at a spot overlooking the town, he was overcome. The snowy mountains loomed above him, and in the valley below, the dark outline of the village was visible. In spots, faint lights glimmered in the darkness, and over all was the vast stillness inherent in the wide-open spaces of nature. Powerfully affected, he rushed home and wrote late into the night.

The next morning, he shared his manuscript with his friend, Franz Gruber, an organist and teacher.

*Carols carry within them an age-old celebration. To sing them is to harmonize with angels and wassailers, wise men and shepherds.*

Within a few hours, Gruber set music to his friend's words. At that night's Mass at the little church, "Silent Night" was first sung, accompanied only by a single guitar, to an undoubtedly hushed and spellbound congregation.

The merry antics of Reverend Hale and his party were perhaps more exuberant, but no less embraced by their audiences.

The benevolent pastor was following the European tradition of caroling, where caroling groups called "waits" roamed to cottage and manor house alike to wish friends and fellow townfolk a Merry Christmas.

According to custom, carolers were rewarded with coins tossed from windows, or with wassail and a snack. Informal groups of peripatetic carolers still carry on the wait tradition, and are often invited inside for cookies and coffee, apple cider, or hot cocoa.

Carols carry within them an age-old celebration. To sing them is to harmonize with angels and wassailers, wise men and shepherds. St. Francis, patron saint of carolers, knew what carolers have rediscovered every year since his time: There is something just a bit transcendent about singing those timeless melodies.

So, in the words of an old Welsh carol: Strike the harp and join the chorus.

He will laugh

Bring your pipes

And bring your drum,

Call the shepherds all to come;

Hasten quick, no time to lose,

Don't forget your dancing shoes.

Frolic we right merrily:

with happy glee,

Yes, and smile, and we will dance,

While he claps his tiny hands.

—*Austrian shepherd's song*

...Therefore bells for Christmas ring, Therefore little children sing

—*Eugene Field*

# stories

There are only two or three human stories, and they go on repeating themselves …

*—Willa Cather*

*A*nd  it came to pass in those days, that there went out a decree from Caesar Augustus, that all the world should be taxed. And all went to be taxed, every one into his own city. And Joseph also went up from Galilee, out of the city of Nazareth, into Judea, unto the city of David, which is called Bethlehem, to be taxed with Mary his espoused wife, being great with child. And so it was, that, while they were there, the days were accomplished that she should be delivered. And she brought forth her firstborn son, and wrapped him in swaddling clothes, and laid him in a manger; because there was no room for them in the inn.

*And there were in the same country shepherds abiding in the field, keeping watch over their flock by night. And, lo, the angel of the Lord came upon them, and the glory of the Lord shone round about them; and they were sore afraid. And the angel said unto them, Fear not: for, behold, I bring you good tidings of great joy, which shall be to all people. For unto you is born this day, in the city of David, a Saviour, which is Christ the Lord. And this shall be a sign unto you: Ye shall find the babe wrapped in swaddling clothes, lying in a manger. And suddenly there was with the angel a multitude of the heavenly host, praising God, and saying, Glory to God in the highest, and on earth peace, good will toward men.*

—Luke 2: 1-14

If it had not been for St. Luke's account of the events of that winter's evening so long ago, we would not be the beneficiaries of so many joyful stories that celebrate this season of peace and goodwill.

The impact of this story was felt around the world. Since that ancient night, countless songs and poems have told, retold, sung, and recited with great joy tales of hope, renewal, and the purest kind of love inspired by that first Christmas story.

One of these legends tells the tale of a small brown bird perched on a beam in a stable in Bethlehem, watching people from many lands come with gifts to worship the newborn Christ Child.

After the visitors departed and the holy family settled down to sleep, the little bird noticed that the fire, built to keep the Christ Child warm, was dying out. The bird flew down and fanned the coals with his wings. Soon the fire became brighter and warmer, and the feathers on the bird's breast began to glow a brilliant red.

The bird stayed by the fire all night, fanning it to keep the blaze bright and the Christ Child warm. Since that first Christmas night, the robin has had a red breast, a symbol of his love for the babe in the manger.

In O. Henry's short story *The Gift of the Magi*, a young husband and wife each, unbeknownest to the other, give up something of great value to themselves in order to buy their beloved a much-desired Christmas gift. She cuts and sells her long, beautiful hair to buy him a watch chain; he sells his watch to buy her a lovely hair comb. The lesson is not the futility of giving, but rather, the sacrifices love compels.

Next to the words of Luke, Charles Dickens' *A Christmas Carol* is surely the most beloved Christmas story of all time.

Though we may have watched, heard, or read it from youth to old age, *A Christmas Carol* still stamps an imprimatur of authenticity on our belief that this is a special time of year. If there is hope for that crotchety old wretch, Ebenezer Scrooge, surely a brighter day awaits us, Every One!

We have taken the lessons embodied in that first Christmas story so much to heart that they not only show up in our literature, but we live them out in our own lives, too.

In an essay called "Blue Christmas," writer Terry Andrews reminisces about Christmas 1958, when he was 11, and he wanted nothing more in the world than the shiny, blue Italian bicycle at Johnston's Hardware on the Hill. He knew, though, that this was

the year his 45-year-old father was going back to college—and that there would likely be no bicycle under the tree.

He decided to give his father his life savings—everything he'd been saving to buy himself that bicycle.

"I ran to my room, and on a piece of paper I wrote, 'Dear Dad, this is for your education.' I carefully folded the paper and in it I put the money I had saved for my bicycle—twelve one-dollar bills," he writes. "He'd never guess in a million years what a shoebox as light as a feather

held. Carefully I wrapped it and put it under the tree."

When his father opened his gift, Andrews recalls, "His eyes seemed to fill with tears...

"[A] realization came over me, suddenly, as I picked up the blue pencils my brother had given me," he writes. "Christmas was more than giving presents, or receiving presents...

"It was my brother stretching his allowance to buy us gifts. It was the care I had put into making those hot pads [for my mother]. It was my sister being there, before she went to college.

We have taken the lessons embodied in that first Christmas story so much to heart that they not only show up in our literature, but we live them out in our own lives, too.

It was my mother bustling in the kitchen, singing "Silent Night," and my father getting out his Bing Crosby record for the umpteenth time. It was carols and cookies and colored lights, a family in a small town on a morning when the snow fell thick and fast. It was love and sharing and being together. It was intangible stuff—memories, tradition, hope. It was catching, for a moment, a glimpse of peace."

# The Visit of St. Nicholas

*'Twas the night before Christmas when all through the house*
*Not a creature was stirring, not even a mouse;*
*The stockings were hung by the chimney with care,*
*In hopes that Saint Nicholas soon would be there.*
*The children were nestled all snug in their beds,*
*While visions of sugarplums danced through their heads.*
*And Mama in her 'kerchief and I in my cap*
*Had just settled our brains for a long Winter's nap.*
*When out on the lawn there arose such a clatter*
*I sprang from my bed to see what was the matter.*

*Away to the window I fled like a flash,*
*Tore open the shutters and threw up the sash.*
*The moon on the breast of the new fallen snow*
*Gave the luster of midday to objects below.*
*When what to my wondering eyes should appear*
*But a miniature sleigh and eight tiny reindeer.*
*With a little old driver so lively and quick*
*I knew in a moment it must be St. Nick.*
*More rapid than Eagles his coursers they came.*
*And he whistled and shouted and called them by name.*
*"Now, Dasher! now, Dancer! now, Prancer! and Vixen!*
*On Comet! on Cupid! on Donder and Blitzen!*
*To the top of the porch! to the top of the wall;*
*Now dash away! dash away! dash away all!"*
*As dry leaves that before the wild hurricane fly*

When they meet with an obstacle mount to the sky,
So up to the housetop the coursers they flew,
With the sleigh full of toys and Saint Nicholas, too.
And then in a twinkle I heard on the roof
The prancing and pawing of each little hoof—
As I drew in my head and was turning around
Down the chimney Saint Nicholas came with a bound.
He was dressed all in furs from his head to his foot,
And his clothes were all tarnished with ashes and soot.
A bundle of toys he had flung on his back
And he looked like a peddler just opening his pack;
His eyes—how they twinkled! His dimples, how merry.
His cheeks were like Roses, his nose like a Cherry!
His droll little mouth was drawn up in a bow,
And the beard on his chin was as white as the snow;
The stump of a pipe he held tight in his teeth,

And the smoke it encircled his head like a wreath;
He had a broad face and a little round belly,
That shook when he laughed like a bowlful of jelly.
He was chubby and plump, a right jolly old elf,
And I laughed when I saw him in spite of myself;
A wink of his eye and a twist of his head
Soon gave me to know I had nothing to dread;
He spoke not a word, but went straight to his work
And filled all the stockings, then turned with a jerk.
And laying his finger aside of his nose
And giving a nod up the chimney he rose.
He sprang to his sleigh, to his team gave a whistle,
And away they all flew like the down of a thistle;
But I heard him exclaim ere he drove out of sight,
"Merry Christmas to all, and to all a good night."

—Clement Clarke Moore

Green under tinsel

Glitter and glow

Appled with baubles

Silver and gold

Spangled with fire

Warm over cold.

—*Laurence Smiths*

It

comes

to stay with

us inside, to be

green life in its green

pride.

—*Paul Engle*

Now in white winter of snowing we get our tree

green hue of growing.

—*Paul Engle*

*...a steaming cup of rich, creamy, sweet, hot cocoa warms the toes, warms the fingers, warms the nose... warms the head... good for the body, good for the soul...*

# feasting

Then I would be slap-dashing home, the gravy smell of the

dinners of others, the bird smell, the brandy,

the pudding and mince, coiling up to my nostrils. . .

—*Dylan Thomas*, A Child's Christmas in Wales, *1954*

Now Christmas is come, let's beat up the drum,
And call all our neighbors together.
And when they appear, let's make them such cheer
As will keep out the wind and the weather.

*—Washington Irving*

## "A feast is made for laughter," says the Book of Ecclesiastes.

There is perhaps no facet of holiday celebration that is more personal, more anticipated, more rich with memories than gathering around the table with family and friends.

Its labors are as sweet as its rewards, because it is not only the eating of the food that is invested with ritual and tradition, it is its preparation, too. As we pull out dog-eared and butter-stained recipe cards and cookbooks, there is great comfort and joy in the chopping, the stirring, the warm aromas coming from the oven as we once again ready for a Christmas feast that feeds both body and spirit.

The Christmas feast serves many purposes. It feeds a hunger for home and floods us with memories of that familiar place.

"Growing up in a military family meant moving around a lot," says an Oregon woman. "It was my mother's stuffing that helped cure our not-so-well-hidden homesickness on our first Christmas in the Philippines. Once Dad carved the bird, we didn't put down our forks until our plates were empty—a second time."

A woman whose mother immigrated to this country from England remembers licking the sweet marzipan filling from the Father Christmas figurine that always adorned her family's Christmas cake.

"Because it just wasn't Christmas without them," she says, "my mother wrote home for the family Christmas cake recipe and her figurine soon after she [came here]."

The much-maligned fruitcake had an entirely different effect on a Washington woman, who loved her mother's fruitcake so much she had her bake a large version of it for her wedding cake and then had a local bakery decorate it with marzipan yellow roses.

"Even though I make it at holiday time," she says, "I still think of it as my wedding cake."

That young woman gave her mother the gift of confidence by asking her to bake her special cake to celebrate one of the most important days of her life; and in turn, her mother showed her love for her daughter by laboring to do it. Indeed, as much as the Christmas feast is an indulgence, it also teaches us to be unselfish, giving us something to share with others.

When we create and maintain Christmas-feast traditions, no matter how simple they may be, we create continuity for generation after generation.

A woman of Norwegian heritage, together with her mother, began to hold the holiday baking sessions held by her grandmother and her grandmother's sisters years ago.

"*Krumkake* (a cone-shaped cookie filled with whipped cream) is our favorite, possibly because it's a necessity to have help," she says, "and it's a good excuse for a get-together. When my granddaughter was only three days old, she attended her very first *krumkake* session!"

In many aspects of life, predictability can be a bane, but when it comes to the traditions of the holiday feast, it is a comfort.

"A timeworn recipe for candied pecans has moved with our family all over the Deep South, tucked safely in the bottom drawer of an antique pine chest," says a Georgia woman. "From January to November it lies there, patiently waiting for that December day when I pull it out for another round of holiday baking."

When we create and maintain Christmas-feast traditions, no matter how simple they may be, we create continuity for generation after generation.

A Minnesota woman remembers her Scandinavian mother and German father joining forces in the kitchen— with flour flying— to make Norwegian *lefse* (a thin, flat, and tender potato bread) to the tune of Bing Crosby's "Silver Bells."

"My father may have been of German extraction," she says, "but he could flip lefse with the best of them."

The culinary fixtures of Christmas, whatever they may be for each of us, provide constancy from year to year, something that can be counted on, a touch of sweetness and warmth. Those qualities are not so different than what we give to and receive from those we love. Perhaps that is why we are compelled each midwinter to feast with friends and family.

When we share a Christmas feast with others, we give them the very best of the season, the very best of any season, the very best of ourselves.

Nothing says Christmas more swe

etly and succinctly than cookies.

"Christmas is coming, and the holidays are coming, and all the children are coming, and all the grand-children are coming, and all their country cousins are coming, and all their uncles and aunts are coming, and every one of these wants their share of Christmas goodies, the Christmas eating and Christmas drinking, the Christmas pies, cakes, puddings and Christmas confections; its bon-bons, nicknacks and its forty thousand sweet things."

— *James W. Parkinson, "Christmas Good Cheer," The Confectioner's Journal, December 1877*

Into the basin put the plums

Stirabout, stirabout, stirabout!

Next the good white flour comes,

Stirabout, stirabout, stirabout!

Sugar and peel and eggs and spice,

Stirabout, stirabout, stirabout!

Mix them and fix them and cook them twice,

Stirabout, stirabout, stirabout!

—*Traditional English verse*

# The following people gave the gift of their talents and resources in creating this book.

### adornment

Molly Culbertson, Candace Ord Manroe, Rebecca Jerdee, Richard Saunders, Craig Kennedy, and Heather Wright Lobdell contributed to the text of this chapter.

Image of wreath on page 10 provided from the Hallmark Design Collection.

### light

Candace Ord Manroe and Rebecca Jerdee contributed to the text of this chapter.

Essay excerpted from *Christmas in the Midwest*, edited by Clarence Andrews,© 1994 Penfield Press.

### worship

Images on page 28, 32, and 33 provided from the Hallmark Design Collection.

Essays excerpted from *Christmas in the Midwest*, edited by Clarence Andrews,© 1994 Penfield Press.

### father Christmas

Heather Lobdell, Candace Ord Manroe, and Gloria Nussbaum contributed to the text of this chapter.

Image on page 46 provided from the Hallmark Design Collection.

### greetings

Nancy A. Fandel, Sally Hopkins, and Nancy Matheny contributed to the text of this chapter.

Images on pages 50-51 and 54-55 provided from the Hallmark Design Collection.

Stamps on pages 56-57 supplied by Stamps 'n' Stuff, West Des Moines, IA

### gifts

Larry Erickson contributed to the text of this chapter.

Images on page 63 and 64 provided from the Hallmark Design Collection.

### songs

Dan Weeks contributed to the text of this chapter.

Original art on pages 68-69 supplied by Hallmark Cards, Inc.

### stories

John Mortimer and Steve Cooper contributed to the text of this chapter.

Images on page 78-79 provided by the Hallmark Design Collection.

Essay excerpted from *Christmas in the Midwest*, edited by Clarence Andrews,© 1994 Penfield Press.

### o Christmas tree

Molly Culbertson, Heather Wright Lobdell, Bob Brenner, Diane C. Arkins, and Linda Joan Smith contributed to the text of this chapter.

### feasting

Julia Martinusen contributed to the text of this chapter.